MY MAMA NAMED ME TOMORROW

My Mama Named Me Tomorrow

BERMUDA

My Mama Named Me Tomorrow
© 2025 Bermuda
ISBN: 979-8-9987811-4-8

Published by Youth Writer's Press
Colton, California
youthwriterspress.com

First Edition, 2025

To request permissions, you may contact the Publisher at
info@youthwriterscamp.com

Printed in the United States of America.

Cover design by Damani Ajamu Berry & Emily Anne Evans
Layout design by Emily Anne Evans / Photon Moment LLC

CONTENTS

vii Foreword

3 Action Maketh Man

6 The Patriot Price

7 The American Scheme

8 Pockets Full of Lint & Zombies in the Streets

9 I'm So Proud of My Big Brother

10 They Sell Me Diamonds from My Own River

11 What Would You Give to feel Safe?

12 Man Always Makes the Best Monsters

13 All in One lifetime

14 Fighting for Life

16 Sole Sacrifice

17 God's Last Gift to Earth

19 Everything Once Was

FOREWORD

Damani has developed into a free thinker, artist & aesthete. He is our son, which we spell sun (son/sun;homophone) because he brings warmth and light into our world. His creative mind and big heart sets him apart. Be regaled by a Poetic interpretation of his life experiences, through allegory, analogy, metaphor and similes.

We are proud of the virtuous man he is and becoming.

Proud Parents
Donetta & Jaa

My Mama Named Me Tomorrow

ACTION MAKETH MAN

God bless the man brave enough to be a man
Willing to let his past self go to become a man he can be
proud of
A man willing to face the consequences of his actions
and stomach answers to questions that needed to be
asked
A man willing to be wrong but irregardless
Relentlessly searching for what's right
Not changing the world to fit his perspective
But changing the world to fit his mind
A man that can't see past his own pain or his own
pleasure is no man at all
That is a boy who can't see past the steering wheel
Knowledge comes from outside and nourishes us
Like the food in our fridge
Food for thought
But peace is the electricity running through the lights
even when it's night
Fair is a fraction 1/2, 1/4, 2/4, 3/4, 4/4
So on and so forth
But peace exists outside in nature like lightning
It doesn't come without clouds
A boy thinks a hurricane comes to take
A man would think it came to wipe the earth clean
This false peace we see on TV
Illustrates to me how we watch these images on mute
and refute any cause that isn't ours
But it also shows that ignorance can't be silenced
Only a man can take responsibility for his future

Peace radiates

Ego regulates

A man's peace shines light where a fool's ego fears to tread

I see ignorance like a beast in pain

I can't heal like my Mother with closed hands or a closed mind

I can't build like my Father if I have a closed heart

I'm the son of a matriarch

I'm not a rest haven for promiscuous women

Nor am I a rehab for broken men

I'm not a nursery for anyone's preconceived notions

Because I belong to me before I'm anyone else's

And any overflow fills the lakes and rivers

When I'm on the clock I am an example of what to do

When I'm off the clock I am liable to be an example of what not to do

But I can only be judged by a man with all the time in the world

Ultimately I practice what I preach as best I can

And I know it

And that is the highest peace any man can achieve

Because if u can't you need to change what you preach

If u feel lost screech

So people can find you

Hit dogs holler

Strays hate collars

Men fail Men fall Men falter but the man that climbs unfazed and unaltered

Occupies a space just beneath his ideals

Still amongst our most praised scholars

Forever a student of life
A man knows the decision was made before any
ultimatums were given
Fluent in the language of action
And aware he alone is the author
And speaking for himself
Because miscommunication
Is the same as death in both campaigns and conquest

THE PATRIOT PRICE

This is to my unborn
Daughter or son
They said their fight
was good
They said their fight
was just
they said their fight
was mine
but my plight
was my own
Since might makes right
They took all I had till even my light
wasn't mine alone
Born here but yall don't want me
If we left you'd be so lonely
If we approached things with open minds
I could open your eyes to looking at things more wholly
But it isn't
Up to me solely
Now I'd be happy just to go
even if it's slow
U don't even want to listen if u cant control me
U don't wanna blame yourself so u pin it on the business
Because u can sue a company like it's a separate entity
You wash your hands with dirty money
And spit on my legacy

THE AMERICAN SCHEME

You rob my country of its resources and gold
Push us into predicaments where we can't say no
You and your constituents divide up the globe
Yet I can't even enter your home
At the core of our country you pick and choose who are
the criminals
Thus we must turn a blind eye to the trouble you get into
Why not let us hide behind your walls
We built them
We had heroes
and you killed them
Unconcerned with safe haven
Yet selling arms to those who would devour our nations
Your only concerns are taxation tax havens vacations
and where to place your base of operations on these
lands that are not yours
Turning peripheral countries into plantations
And draining the brains of those gifted enough to
change the situation
I talked to my girlfriend who is Haitian and she opened
my eyes to the illustrations you paint on all the world
stages
You say this is the land of opportunity
A home for the brave
Watched over by lady liberty
You say this is the place to be but we can't come
Because the brave come home and sleep on the streets
next to the ones who cant find any opportunity
as they learned one can fly too high here
And fall
Real hard

POCKETS FULL OF LINT & ZOMBIES IN THE STREETS

A.K.A GO RESEARCH HOW THE WEALTH IS DISTRIBUTED IN THIS COUNTRY— IT'S ACTUALLY INSANE

I can't afford to agree to disagree anymore
It's up till it's stuck
like it's crawling out the floor
through the windows through the door
You made monsters out of the poor
Helicopters on the roof
That sound like a hell hounds roar
Eating off plates with 3 different forks
Still with manners so poor
I shudder at the thought of what hell has in store
I wonder if you ever had to endure
A storm in your stomach
A sword at your gullet
The ballot or the bullet
The ballad of the bullet
And some will face the music sooner than others
And the bass will hit your face like thunder
Their ships go to space in less time than it takes for a
healthy slumber
In endless castles that shine like summer
For people with class and cleaning staffs
Y'all are some sinners in silk

I'M SO PROUD OF MY BIG BROTHER

We aren't blood but the bond we share is much better
You've never treated me like an outsider
Even when you lit fires that burned away my ignorance
Because when you witness massacres like I did
No one is innocent
I was chasing trouble
laughing under rubble when you found me
And you too were in ruins when I found you
You simply took my seat in class
it was no profound thing
But soon I couldn't see the forest through the trees
without you next to me
Living for the warm blood of the battlefield
But whenever we hung out after school I always had a meal
U showed me that even artists will wage war
When something is worth fighting for
And I like to think that I showed you that there's more to life than the path other people have already explored
I owe so much of what I am and more
to everyone who made me feel at home when
I knocked on your door
Thank you guys so much

THEY SELL ME DIAMONDS FROM MY OWN RIVER

The human mind is like a river
If you dive into the divine blindly even the
coldest blooded killer will shiver
The enchanting prismatic glimmer
Flowing from the mountains that shimmer
All the thoughts swimming around in my head
and even the ones I don't remember
Shape the person I'm becoming
But the Greek philosopher Heraclitus said you will never
step in the same river twice
I can build a cobblestone bridge
whenever you cross my mind
But if you can't go with the flow
You will get left behind
I know from firsthand experience
That I can hold your hand and walk on water with you
But I can't make you believe
Still you drink endlessly
Yet you purify anything that makes it me
And who does that help
When you expect me to bottle up my beliefs
So you can enjoy my presence with a refreshing sense of
relief
It seems to make sense to everyone except me because
everyone makes a couple dollars off the flavor
So they put me in a box and then put me in a freezer
And save me for later
But the human mind is like a river
And if I let myself freeze I might never melt

WHAT WOULD YOU GIVE TO FEEL SAFE?

How much money do you need to feel free
Is your head barely above water
Does it rise like the tide every week
Because they never let anyone be free for free
And some of us have been paying for it ever since
One man sells his enemies into slavery
Because he truly believes they don't deserve to be free
Only for the man he sold them to
To be the man that funds the war and
profits off it
Because he secretly believes
Both sides are no better than beasts
Another man will sell his liberty to his enemy's enemy
for safety
Only to end up at the end of his blade
Dissected on his plate
Money has no owners because cash is king
Or at least cash rules everything around me
Money isn't a loyal woman
She came here with you
but she's gonna leave here with me
Then there's me
Free to water my grass however I please
It really is all about the simple things

MAN ALWAYS MAKES THE BEST MONSTERS

I don't believe in ghouls gnomes nor goblins vampires and minotaurs
Trolls dragons or mummies
Beholders zombies and gorgons
Skin walkers la llorona chupacabra
Baba yaga jörmungandr
I dont believe in Mothman slenderman or orcs
I don't believe in Jorögumo Werewolves Wendigos
Still as I look out across the open sea in these dark times
All I see are glowing eyes staring back at me
But that could only mean that all the monsters around me are human

ALL IN ONE LIFETIME

I am consumed by things I can't control
Fortune favors the bold
But I crave to grow old in a profession
Where most people don't
I want to have fun
Because everything we learn about the world happens in
one lifetime
And humanity hates change
We crave organization
stillness stability
freedom legacy
and art
It is in our ability
to feel 2 separate things
at the same time
and our inability to admit it
or reconcile the differences
that this kind of ignorance
flourishes
as everything we learn about the world everything we
learn about ourselves
everything we learn about each other
all happens in one lifetime
Slashing education is the lubricant for the manipulation
as the revolution can't be televised
It's too real for radio if we can't fight for our freedom
here
Tomorrow our children will fight
It is our orphans and widows that will become warriors

FIGHTING FOR LIFE

Fight?
Fight for what?
You have nothing
I fight because I am nothing
and I want something
So give me liberty or death
Because I want everything if I have to take it
and I won't even let you have what's left
Send your cards to my carcass
you left me for dead
If I went to the circus
Clowns are what I'd expect
With all due respect
you speak like an elect
and yet not an intellect
The architect of your own demise retrospect
You speak like a man without anything to protect
yet you don't protest
Putting others down because you alone don't impress
It makes my stomach so upset
to see you so full of regrets
I pour my pain into cassettes
Because I have an old soul
I've lived a short life with high highs and low lows
when sweat beat my brow
I had no choice but to grow
Talking to walls with ears hearing no voice but my own
sick of missing history
I'll make it from this point on

God please pull us into our purpose
I don't want to make it out of my environment alone
I know I'll be fine on my own
but that's not the future I want
I'm not saying I won't
But I don't want to have to
You might see me once in 50 years or you might see me
every day
I live my life like comets
flying through space
Baby pump your brakes
I aint got the kinda thrills you chase
Grass grows in silence and
I been growing since they pulled me out the vase

SOLE SACRIFICE

I would have died for you
and you would have let me
I'm not here to make you comfortable
I'll leave this earth behind
when I'm good and ready
All is forgiven
But the shambles of bridge
Is just where you left it
But you demand that I rebuild it
I've been the bigger man so much
my head hit the ceiling
When I enter buildings
But you don't care about my feelings
You tried to put your arm around me
because my shoulders cold
But don't mind me I'm chilling
It's your life story
And I was sure you could pick a better villain
Than your children
Nothing less than
The objects of your affection
In desperate need of protection
From your obsession

GOD'S LAST GIFT TO EARTH

Blood of my blood
Kin of my kin
What's yours is mine
And mine is mine
It's tradition
One white lie
Isn't a sin
It's in the repetition
I tell u what the good book ain't telling
Your heavenly father sent down the stairs to heaven
But it landed in one man's backyard
Michael told him this is for all gods children
When Michael left him
The man built walls and weapons
The rich were the only ones he let in exchange for gold
and jewels
Because he believed the poor were fools and the stairs
were his to use
He gained the world and all it cost was his sleep
All his finest linen and silk sheets
That were far from cheap
Protection under his pillowcase because he was scared of
the sheep
Pre emptive punishment he called justice
Protestors stood outside with picket signs that said "just
us"
Michael looked down at the crowd and was disgusted
The man looked out at the crowd and saw his walls were
busted

That's when he started running
Up and he realized that the stairs went nowhere
He was so hurt that nobody cared about how betrayed he
felt
He was so concerned about how everyone else got into
heaven and he forgot about himself

EVERYTHING ONCE WAS

I wish I was God again
Not because I have a problem with the way the man
upstairs is running things
But because I can remember counting infinite on my
fingers in seconds
I can almost remember the smell of heaven
But back then I was just a mural on the wall
After all as I was made in his image
Today I woke up a mortal man washing dishes
So u say
You will always be there
because you will always care
But if you don't let me be me
and by that
I mean a sensitive soul you too will end up with all the
pain that I buried and even when I dig you up
You won't be there to hold me
My Papa told me
At his father's funeral
He cried because he knew that in the darkest night
at his darkest time he could scream
till he went blind and his father
would no longer come running
I feel like I'm running in circles
And I keep feeling feelings and letting them go and the
cycles keep speeding up so much that I'm losing control
I can't catch a breath in this vortex
while I fight for my soul
So I must endure

More
It's embedded in the words that you choose when we
speak
It makes me think you think that I'm not brave
That I'm not bold
That If I don't harden my heart to the hunger of the
world
I won't grow old
But I'm here to say
I've seen the future
And if I do
I won't grow at all
From the apple of both your eyes
From tomorrow with love

ABOUT THE AUTHOR

One night my mother prayed that her son would be born healthy and safely. Though, at the same time, she was ready to have her body back and the next morning I was born with the Sunrise. The name Damani translates to tomorrow. I am Damani Ajamu Berry, also known as Bermuda, and I've spent my entire life writing these poems. Currently, I am a senior at California State University of San Bernardino majoring in Sociology, therefore at the core of this book in each poem there is a passion for conversation about society. Through critique and imagery I hope that this can open a dialogue between people where they reach outside their comfort zone and open their minds to different perspectives.

youthwriterspress.com

A program of Youth Writer's Camp, Inc., Youth Writer's Press exists to create a safe space where young voices are heard, valued, and amplified. We are dedicated to producing and publishing work that allows youth to share their truths with the world. Our mission is to equip the next generation of writers with the resources, confidence, and platform to turn their stories into lasting works that resound far beyond the page.

youthwriterscamp.com

This book was created as part of Youth Writer's Camp, Inc., a nonprofit organization whose mission is to motivate communities to redefine hope for young people through mentoring, enrichment, and creativity.

In our workshops and programs, we blend literacy enrichment, social-emotional development, and creative entrepreneurship — using writing as a tool for healing, growth, and community connection.

Youth Writer's Camp Values:

COURAGE Creating the strength to face challenges with confidence.

RESILIENCE Creating the ability to bounce back and keep moving forward.

EMPATHY Creating connections by truly understanding others' feelings.

AUTHENTICITY Creating a space where you can be your true self without masks.

TRANSPARENCY Creating an atmosphere of openness and honesty, where vulnerability is valued.

ENTERPRISING Creating opportunities through innovation and a dynamic mindset.